101 WAYS TO KNOW IF YOUR CAT IS IRISH

How To Talk To Your Cat About Their Secret Life
and the Romance and Mystery of Being Irish,
A Funny Cat Book and The Perfect Gift for Cat
Lovers and Those Who Love Ireland

Seamus Mullarkey

101 Ways To Know If Your Cat Is Irish

Copyright © 2023 by Seamus Mullarkey

All rights reserved.

Plain Scribes Press

www.plainscribespress.com

DON'T MISS THIS SPECIAL BONUS

GET YOUR FREE BOOK TODAY...

IT'S SO SIMPLE – AND TOTALLY FREE!
– SCAN THE CODE OR CLICK THE LINK....

subscribepage.io/7565d5

Is your cat dreaming of Ireland?

INTRODUCTION

Could your cat be Irish? Are there things about it that could only be explained by a truly Irish temperament? Imagine your cat enjoying a pint of Irish catnip beer, reciting poetry by Ireland's own W.B Yeats, or even dancing a jig to traditional Irish music. The truth is, your cat may have more in common with the likes of Saoirse Ronan or Bono than you ever imagined.

But don't just take our word for it, this book is packed with 101 ways to tell if your cat is truly Irish. From their love of a good cup o' tea, to their innate ability to charm the pants off anyone they meet, we've got the inside scoop on all the telltale signs of a true Irish cat.

So, grab your cat and a bowl of shamrock-shaped treats, and join us as we explore the Emerald Isle through the eyes of your very own Irish feline. We'll discover the rich culture and traditions that make Ireland so beloved. Who knows, you may even learn a thing or two about your cat's true origins. So, whether your cat's name is Fluffy or Finnegan, you're about to discover that their purr-sonality could be far more linked to the Emerald Isle than you ever could have imagined.

However, don't book a trip to Ireland with your cat just yet! You need to be sure, which is why I've created this highly scientific book that has been rigorously tested under laboratory conditions. You see, there are 101 ways for you to know for sure if you should change Fluffy's name to "Sean" or "Bridget." Read on, and you may discover that your cat's love for all things Irish may be more than fur deep. So, let's savor the wonders of Ireland and its culture from the comfort of your home and in the company of your dear, darling "puss."

1

It treasures its food bowl
as if it's a pot of gold.

2

Its Irish eyes are always smiling.

3

It won't back down from a fight.

4

You can usually find it sitting in the pub.

5

It wants you to write a book about it as special as the Book of Kells.

6

It's always on the lookout for the end of the rainbow!

7

It has long legs suitable for a good Riverdance.

8

It demands a cat tower taller than Blarney Castle.

9

It acts like it's Bono from U2.

10

It's mad for 'the drink.'

11

It dreams of listening to the waves of
The Irish Sea.

12

It wants you to read it an old Irish fairytale.

13

It has been known to harbor a grudge.

14

It has a mean left hook.

15

It's always up to some '*divilment.*'

16

It can talk your ear off with its gift of the gab!

17

It longs to lounge on the lush green grass of the Emerald Isle.

18

It's always up for a sing-song.

19

It's not shy around strangers.

20

When you talk about saluting the flag, it thinks of this one.

21

It looks fantastic in a kilt.

22

Its coat is as dark and smooth as a glass of Guinness.

23

It's not afraid of a hard day's work.

24

It's usually up for a good time and lots of 'craic.'

25

It always says its prayers
before it goes to bed.

26

It refers to the television as "the Telly."

27

It gets shy when you flatter it.

28

You know it would enjoy old-
fashioned ceili dancing.

29

It's not afraid of a challenge and punches above its weight.

30

It's in no hurry to get there on time. – "ah sure, it'll keep...'

31

It plays tricks on you like a mischievous little leprechaun.

32

Its Irish granny taught it to always say "Thank You!"

33

It loves dairy products from the Emerald Isle.

34

It has a warm heart.

35

It's always on the hunt for a shamrock.

36

It's most comfortable down on the farm.

37

It doesn't knead biscuits, it makes
Irish soda bread!

38

It can pronounce Saoirse Ronan's name correctly, as well as other Irish girls' names like 'Ailbhe' or 'Meadhbh'.

39

It wants to taste a hearty Irish stew
made the good old-fashioned way...

40

Like the Irish poet William Butler Yeats, it thinks "a stranger is just a friend you haven't met..."

41

It yearns to gaze at the majestic Cliffs of Moher.

42

Its family bonds are strong as can be.

43

It likes nothing better than to watch Liam Neeson films.

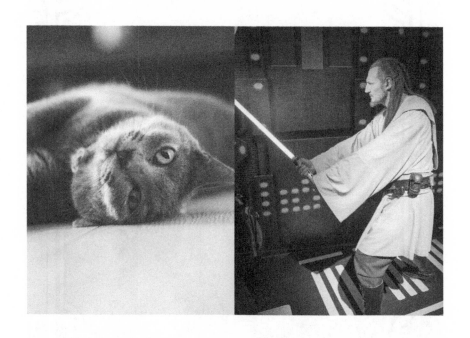

44

It looks like an ancient "Irish druid," full of wisdom.

44

45

It believes the Irish saying "<u>Two</u> cats on a journey shorten the road."

46

It's mesmerized by harp music.

47

It believes in the fairy folk.

48

It. doesn't mind a spot of rain, "Sure it makes the grass greener."

49

It fears mammy's wooden spoon more than thunder and lightning.

50

It dreams of roaming the streets in Dublin.

51

It doesn't like to lay in the sun for too long, in case it freckles...

52

It wants to steal some of your Irish breakfast.

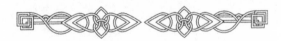

53

It'll watch soccer but it prefers the mad thrills of Gaelic football.

54

Its ancestors emigrated far and wide.

55

You find it dancing a jig in the kitchen in the middle of the night.

56

It would charm the birds out of the trees.

57

It bundles up well on chilly mornings – there wasn't much central heating back in Ireland...

58

It loves its mammy more than anything.

59

It sneaks a peek at your books about Ireland.

60

It loves those sad Irish songs: "Sure they'd bring a tear to a glass eye."

61

It's 'not one for gossip' but always keeps an eye on the neighbors.

62

Its Irish eyes would melt even the hardest of hearts.

63

When it sleeps, it dreams of dancing
a reel in the moonlight.

64

It always has time for a cup of tea.

65

It's on the run from someone named Mac or Murphy.

66

It knows you can't beat the warmth of an open fire.

67

It gives you 'that look' when you play Enya's music.

68

It dresses up in its best for Sunday mass.

69

It likes nothing better than hanging around with 'the lads.'

70

You just know it's going to curse like a sailor at the vet's.

71

It is proud of its ancestry.

72

When it's mad, it hisses, "I'll give you something to cry about!"

73

It acts annoyed when you call it a "British shorthair."

74

It howls like a banshee at 4am.

75

It says, "Kiss me, I'm Irish!"

76

You've found it taking "*selfies*" to post as @EmeraldKitty2027.

77

It sulks when you watch any of those British costume dramas on TV.

78

It cocks its ears when they play an Irish tune.

79

You spot a shamrock-shaped marking on its fur.

80

It drinks more milk if you sprinkle some Lucky Charms on top.

81

It comes from a very large family.

82

It purrs when you serve potatoes.

83

If it's a boy, its name is
Paddy, Mick, or Joe.

84

If it's a girl, it's called Kathleen, Mary, or Bridget.

85

It goes drinking with mice instead of chasing them.

86

It stands up when they play the Irish anthem.

87

It lets you dress it up on St. Patrick's Day.

88

It pees all over your English Ivy.

89

It runs across the yard when you mention a trip to Ireland.

90

It meows along to the melody of Galway Bay.

91

It gazes longingly at any Irish
pictures you have in the house.

92

It wakes you up early because it's "on Irish time."

93

When it's annoyed it makes a noise like bagpipes.

94

It makes you laugh with its shenanigans!

95

It loves when they play
"Danny Boy."

96

Its granny cooked on a cast iron stove.

97

It has the luck of the Irish and wins
every time.

98

It has a feisty temper!

99

It insists it once met a leprechaun outside Killarney.

100

You think you heard it whisper "Erin Go Bragh."

101

It knows there'll be a pot of gold at the end of the rainbow.

Slán go Fóill (slawn guh Fohhl)...
See You Later...

CONCLUSION

After a journey through the rolling hills of Ireland, a walk along the Cliffs of Moher, and lazy afternoons listening to traditional Irish music, this feline tour of Ireland has come to an end. Just how Irish did your kitty turn out to be? Do they have a penchant for potatoes, more than the typical bowl of kibble? Or, do they go mad for some old-time ceili dancing? Perhaps your four-legged companion has surprised you with just how how much they love the haunting melody of the uileann pipes! In that case, you could certainly look forward to embracing the craic and learning the ways of the Emerald Isle together.

And never fear if any of the traits came as a shock to both of you – there are always new and exciting lessons to be learned, whether it be from the Irish or your cat. They may be onto something with their love of a fine Irish smoked salmon...

DON'T MISS THIS SPECIAL BONUS

GET YOUR FREE BOOK TODAY...

IT'S SO SIMPLE – AND TOTALLY FREE!
– SCAN THE CODE OR CLICK THE LINK....

subscribepage.io/7565d5

Please leave a review...

If this book brought you a few moments of pleasure, I'd be so grateful if you took just a few moments to leave a review on the book's Amazon page.

You can get to the review page simply by following the link

or QR code below. Thanks!

Purrr-leeze leave a review!

About the Author

A cat fanatic and book lover, I write fascinating books about our beloved kitties and how they've shaped our world.

— If you love cats, you'll love my books —

So, why not join my "Cats of the World" fan club? You can read all my new books FOR FREE?

AND... You'll get a free bonus book, "How to Speak French With Your Cat"...

SIMPLY SCAN THE CODE OR CLICK THE LINK TO JOIN!
There's no cost to you
subscribepage.io/7565d5

More from Seamus Mullarkey

Would you like to read more of my books???
Just click or scan below...

**SCAN TO VIEW
DETAILS...**

More from Seamus Mullarkey

Would you like to read more of my books???
Just click or scan below...

**SCAN TO VIEW
DETAILS...**

More from Seamus Mullarkey

Would you like to read more of my books???
Just click or scan below...

**SCAN TO VIEW
DETAILS...**

More from Seamus Mullarkey

Would you like to read more of my books???
Just click or scan below...

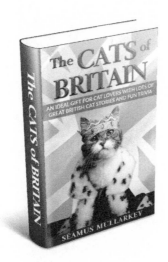

**SCAN TO VIEW
DETAILS...**

... and there's lots more to come ...

Scan the code or click the link so you get notified the minute I release a new book...

SCAN TO FOLLOW ME

Made in United States
North Haven, CT
07 June 2023

37472039R00075